Amazing Elephants

Charlotte Guillain

Raintree

Raintree is an imprint of Capstone Global Library Limited, a company incorporated in England and Wales having its registered office at 7 Pilgrim Street, London, EC4V 6LB – Registered company number: 6695582

www.raintreepublishers.co.uk
myorders@raintreepublishers.co.uk

Text © Capstone Global Library Limited 2013
First published in hardback in 2013
Paperback edition first published in 2014
The moral rights of the proprietor have been asserted.

Edited by Daniel Nunn, Rebecca Rissman, and Catherine Veitch
Designed by Victoria Allen
Picture research by Mica Brancic
Production by Victoria Fitzgerald
Originated by Capstone Global Library Ltd
Printed and bound in China by CTPS

ISBN 978 1 406 26078 6 (hardback)
17 16 15 14 13
10 9 8 7 6 5 4 3 2 1

ISBN 978 1 406 26085 4 (paperback)
18 17 16 15 14
10 9 8 7 6 5 4 3 2 1

British Library Cataloguing in Publication Data
Guillain, Charlotte.
Amazing elephants. -- (Walk on the wild side)
599.6'7-dc23
A full catalogue record for this book is available from the British Library.

Acknowledgements
We would like to thank the following for permission to reproduce photographs:Alamy p. 15 (© Steve Bloom Images); Getty Images pp. 7 (National Geographic/Dr. John Michael Fay) 9 (Peter Arnold/Martin Harvey), 25 (Oxford Scientific/David Cayless); Nature Picture Library pp. 4 (© Andy Rouse), 8 (© Edwin Giesbers), 11 (© Tony Heald), 12 (© Jabruson), 14 (© Peter Blackwell), 17 (© Ben Osborne), 18 (© Karl Ammann), 20 (© Peter Blackwell), 21 (© Anup Shah), 23 (© Charlie Summers), 24 (© Lisa Hoffner), 26 (© Andy Rouse), 27 (© Anup Shah), 28 (© Vivek Menon), 29 (© Andy Rouse); Shutterstock pp. 5 (Rich Carey), 10 (Stephane Bidouze), 13 (© Cucumber Images), 16 (© Johan Swanepoel), 19 (Jonathan Pledger), 22 (© SouWest Photography).

Cover photograph of an elephant calf reproduced with permission of Shutterstock (© FWStupidio).

We would like to thank Michael Bright for his invaluable help in the preparation of this book.

Every effort has been made to contact copyright holders of material reproduced in this book. Any omissions will be rectified in subsequent printings if notice is given to the publisher.

Some words are shown in bold, **like this**. You can find out what they mean by looking in the glossary.

Contents

Introducing elephants. 4

Where do elephants live? 6

What do elephants look like? 8

Enormous ears. 10

Trunk power .12

Terrible tusks 14

Eating and drinking. 16

Life in a herd 18

Matriarchs .20

Elephant calves. 22

Keeping in touch. 24

Elephants never forget!. 26

Life for an elephant 28

Glossary. 30

Find out more 31

Index 32

Introducing elephants

The elephant is the largest animal living on land, but it is also very gentle and **intelligent**. There are three different **species** of elephant: Asian, African bush, and African forest elephants.

Asian elephants

African bush
elephants

Where do elephants live?

Asian elephants live in India, Sri Lanka, and parts of Southeast Asia. African forest elephants live in **rainforests** in West and Central Africa. African bush elephants live on the **savannah**, in many parts of Africa.

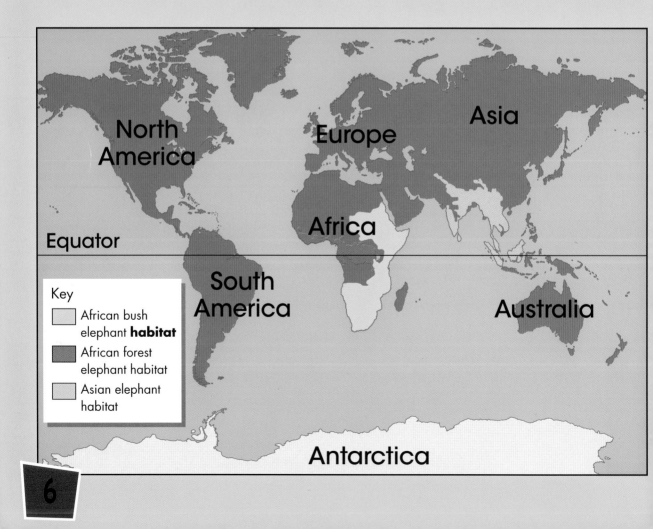

North America

Europe

Asia

Equator

Africa

Key
- African bush elephant **habitat**
- African forest elephant habitat
- Asian elephant habitat

South America

Australia

Antarctica

African forest
elephant

What do elephants look like?

African bush elephants are the largest **species**. They can be up to 4 metres tall. That's over two times the height of an adult man. All elephants have thick, wrinkled grey-brown skin that hangs in folds.

Did you know?
The heaviest elephant ever recorded was a huge 7,500 kilograms. That's as heavy as a small lorry.

Elephants can kneel on their back legs.

Enormous ears

Elephants have huge ears. African bush elephants have much bigger ears than Asian elephants. African forest elephants have more rounded ears than bush elephants.

Asian elephant

Did you know?

African bush elephants can get very hot on the **savannah**. They flap their large ears to help them stay cool.

Trunk power

Elephants can use their trunks to push or lift very heavy objects. But they can also grip and pick up tiny things. Elephants use their trunks to help them cool down. They suck water up their trunks and spray it over themselves.

Asian elephant

Terrible tusks

Most African elephants and some Asian elephants have tusks. Tusks are very long teeth that grow when the elephant loses its baby teeth. Elephants use their tusks to dig for food or strip bark off trees to eat.

African elephant

tusk

African
elephants

Male elephants sometimes use
their tusks to fight each other.

Eating and drinking

Elephants eat grass, roots, leaves, bark, and fruit. These big animals need to eat huge amounts of food to get enough energy. They use their trunks to squirt water and put food into their mouths.

African elephant

Did you know?

Elephants can drink up to 150 litres of water every day. That's the same as drinking 264 pints of milk!

African elephant

Life in a herd

Elephants live in family groups, called **herds**. Herds are made up of related female elephants and their babies. Adult male elephants leave the herd and either live alone or in small groups with other males.

There are usually around ten elephants in a herd.

African elephants

African elephant

Male elephants are called bulls.

Matriarchs

Female elephants are called cows. Each **herd** is led by an older cow, called a **matriarch**. When a matriarch dies, the cow who is most closely related to her becomes the next matriarch.

African elephants

African elephants

The matriarch is very experienced and can show the rest of the herd where to find food and water.

Elephant calves

Female elephants can be pregnant for **18 to 22 months**. Mothers usually only have one baby at a time, called a calf. The **matriarch** teaches her daughters how to care for their calves.

Calves drink milk for around two years.

African elephants

All the elephants in the **herd** help to care for the calves.

African elephants

Keeping in touch

Elephants in a **herd** are very good at **communicating**. They use their senses of sound, touch, and smell. Elephants can make a low rumbling sound that travels over a long distance to keep in touch with each other.

Elephants touch trunks to communicate.

African elephants

African bush elephant

25

Elephants never forget!

Elephants have very good memories. A **matriarch** can remember the way to a water hole many kilometres away, even if she hasn't been there for years.

African elephants

African
elephants

Did you know?

Older elephants pass
on their knowledge
to the younger
elephants in a **herd**
so the herd can keep
the memory going.

Life for an elephant

Elephants are amazing animals. People are still only starting to learn how **intelligent** they are. But elephants are under threat! Humans hunt elephants for their tusks and their **habitat** is getting smaller. We need to protect this magnificent animal.

elephant tusk

Did you know?
Elephants can live for around 65 years.

African elephant

Glossary

communicate pass on and share information

habitat natural home for an animal or plant

herd group of elephants

intelligent clever

matriarch older female who leads a herd

rainforest area of forest with tall trees and a lot of rain

savannah area of grassland found in many parts of Africa south of the Sahara Desert

species type of animal

Find out more

Books

Elephants, James Maclaine (Usborne, 2011)

Elephant vs. Rhinoceros, Isabel Thomas (Raintree, 2007)

Face to Face with Elephants, Beverly and Dereck Joubert (National Geographic, 2008)

Reasons to Care about Elephants, Mary Firestone (Enslow, 2010)

Websites

gowild.wwf.org.uk/regions/africa-fact-files/ african-elephant
gowild.wwf.org.uk/regions/asia-fact-files/ sumatran-elephant
The World Wildlife Fund website has these fact files on elephants.

kids.nationalgeographic.com/kids/animals/ creaturefeature/african-elephant/
The National Geographic website has information on many animals, including African elephants.

Index

African bush elephants 4,
    5, 6, 8, 10, 25
African forest elephants
    4, 6, 7, 10
Asian elephants 4, 6, 10,
    13, 14

bulls 19

calves 22–23
communication 24–25,
    30
cooling down 11, 12
cows 20

ears 10, 11

fighting 15
food 14, 16, 21

habitats 6, 28, 30
herds 18, 20, 21, 23, 24, 27,
    30

intelligence 4, 28, 30

kneeling 9

lifespan 29

matriarchs 20, 21, 22, 26,
    30
memory 26–27
milk 22

pregnancy 22

savannah 6, 11, 30
senses 24
size 8
skin 8
species of elephant 4, 30

teeth 14
trumpeting 25
trunks 12, 16, 24